DK READERS

Level 3

Level 4

A Note to Parents

DK READERS is a compelling program for beginning readers, designed in conjunction with leading literacy experts, including Dr. Linda Gambrell, Distinguished Professor of Education at Clemson University. Dr. Gambrell has served as president of the National Reading Conference, the College Reading Association, and the International Reading Association.

Beautiful illustrations and superb full-color photographs combine with engaging, easy-to-read stories to offer a fresh approach to each subject in the series. Each DK READER is guaranteed to capture a child's interest while developing his or her reading skills, general knowledge, and love of reading.

The five levels of DK READERS are aimed at different reading abilities, enabling you to choose the books that are exactly right for your child:

Pre-level 1: Learning to read
Level 1: Beginning to read
Level 2: Beginning to read alone
Level 3: Reading alone
Level 4: Proficient readers

The "normal" age at which a child begins to read can be anywhere from three to eight years old. Adult participation through the lower levels is very helpful for providing encouragement, discussing storylines, and sounding out unfamiliar words.

No matter which level you select, you can be sure that you are helping your child learn to read, then read to learn!

LONDON, NEW YORK, MUNICH,
MELBOURNE, and DELHI

Series Editor Deborah Lock
Art Editor Mary Sandberg
U.S. Editor John Searcy
Production Editor Siu Chan
Production Erika Pepe
Picture Researcher Harriet Mills
Jacket Designer Rachael Foster

Reading Consultant
Linda Gambrell, Ph.D.

First American Edition, 2008
08 09 10 11 12 10 9 8 7 6 5 4 3 2 1
Published in the United States by DK Publishing
375 Hudson Street, New York, New York 10014

Published in Great Britain by Dorling Kindersley Limited

DK books are available at special discounts when purchased in bulk
for sales promotions, premiums, fund-raising, or educational use.
For details, contact:
DK Publishing Special Markets
375 Hudson Street
New York, New York 10014
SpecialSales@dk.com

A catalog record for this book is available
from the Library of Congress.
ISBN: 978-0-7566-3751-4 (Paperback)
ISBN: 978-0-7566-3750-7 (Hardcover)

Color reproduction by Colourscan, Singapore
Printed and bound in China by L Rex Printing Co., Ltd.

The publisher would like to thank the following for their kind
permission to reproduce their photographs:
(Key: a=above; b=below/bottom; c=center; l=left; r=right; t=top)
African Conservation Foundation: Arend de Haas 46; **Alamy Images:** JTB
Photo Communications, Inc. 27; Khaled Kassem 19tr; Ian Laker 33; Photostall
28bl; Simone van den Berg 28br; **Ardea:** Pat Morris 13tr; **Kate Arnold:** 43; **C.
Chambers:** 42tl; **Corbis:** Gallo Images/Martin Harvey 13br; Kennan Ward 6br;
DK Images: Franklin Park Zoo, Boston 41br; The Jane Goodall Institute 11br;
Rough Guides 31br; Twycross Zoo, Atherstone, Leicestershire 25br; Jerry Young
5tl; **FLPA:** Frans Lanting 16bl; Minden Pictures/Gerry Ellis 7, 26br; Minden
Pictures/Cyril Ruoso/JH Editorial 9; Jurgen & Christine Sohns 3; R & M Van
Nostrand 5c; Terry Whittaker 5tr; **Getty Images:** Pius Utomi Ekpei/AFP 34b, 35;
Hoang Dinh Nam/AFP 29tr; The Image Bank/Michael Melford 15tr; The Image
Bank/Karl Ammann 21br; Minden Pictures/Gerry Ellis 39cr; Minden Pictures/
Cyril Ruoso/JH Editorial 8; **Courtesy Great Ape Trust of Iowa/www.
greatapetrust.org:** 20, 21c, 22, 23br, 23tr, 24, 25t; **iStockphoto.com:** Chanyut
Sribua-rawd 26tl; **The Jane Goodall Institute/www.janegoodall.org:** Brian
Keating 6tl; **Last Refuge:** Cameron Hansen/www.lastrefuge.co.uk 31tr; **National
Geographic Image Collection:** Hugo Van Lawick 10, 12; **naturepl.com:** Anup
Shah 18; **NREL National Renewable Energy Laboratory:** 14tl; **Photolibrary:**
David Courtenay 17; **Photoshot/NHPA:** Mark Bowler 19br; Martin Harvey 32tl,
37tl (inset), 38-39, 40, 41bl; **Science Photo Library:** Tony Camacho 45br; **Still
Pictures:** Martin Harvey 37c; **Wildlife Conservation Society/www.wcs.org:**
Naomi Cohen 42b; Dave Lucas 47tr; Jacqui Sunderland-Groves 45t.
All other images © Dorling Kindersley Limited
For more information see: www.dkimages.com

Discover more at
www.dk.com

Contents

 READERS

READING
3
ALONE

Ape
Adventures

Written by Catherine Chambers

DK Publishing

Family of apes

Tourists gape at apes in zoos and in the wild. Scientists study them in forests and laboratories. Viewers watch ape antics on television screens, but why are we so fascinated by them?

Perhaps it's because apes seem so much like us. They cuddle their young, build shelters, and some even make tools. Apes can tell each other what they feel. In the following adventures, apes show what they think about us, too.

The stories take us to parts of Africa and Asia where apes live in hot tropical and subtropical forests. However, they also live in great danger from hunters and illegal traders, and their forests are being destroyed by farmers and loggers. The survival of apes lies in our hands. ❖

Small Apes

Lar gibbon

Lesser apes, also known as gibbons, spend their lives in trees. The largest kind of gibbon is the siamang.

Siamang

Big Apes

The four great apes are the bonobo, chimpanzee, gorilla, and orangutan.

Chimpanzee

Bonobo

Orangutan

Gorilla

Getting to know you

Who is Jane?
Jane Goodall first went to Africa in 1957. There, she worked with Louis Leakey, who studied animal and human behavior. Jane studied many chimpanzees in the Gombe Stream Game Reserve, in Tanzania.

Jane sat quietly on a high peak in East Africa. The light was hazy in the heat. Thick forest and bushes lined the hollows and hills. Jane stared down at a clump of msulula trees.

"There, Rashidi! You see them?"

The park ranger could see a mother chimpanzee and her three children.

A balanced diet
Chimpanzees live in Africa's forests and grassy savannahs. In these areas, they find plenty of leaves and fruit to eat. They also eat small monkeys.

The mother and her young chimp were plucking handfuls of round, juicy fruits.

"See, there to the right?" Jane said. "Her two teenage sons are learning to hunt that small monkey!"

"In a few years, they'll be ready to find food on their own," said Rashidi.

Older chimp mothers often accept younger mothers into their group. They then share childcare duties.

Jane moved quietly down the slope to get closer. Suddenly, she slipped and crashed through the scratchy bushes. The noise echoed all around the valley. The chimps screeched and scampered off. Jane sighed with frustration. The chimps would never let her get close to them.

Every night, chimps make new nests. They usually make them in trees by bending the branches and gathering leaves.

The air cooled suddenly. The great East African sky changed to a deeper blue, then to a blazing orange, and then to pink. As the sun set, the chimpanzees made sleeping nests in the trees. It was time for Jane and Rashidi to pack up for the day.

Back at the camp, Jane sat down to write in her chimpanzee diary. Before she could write anything, an excited voice made her jump. It was Dominic, a member of her team.

"Jane! You'll never guess what I saw! A chimpanzee, here in the camp! He was eating palm nuts from our trees. Then he stole some bananas from the table."

"What did he look like?" Jane asked.

"He was very large and had long white hairs around his chin," replied Dominic.

"I know him!" cried Jane. "It's the one I call David Greybeard. At last I have a chance to get close to a chimp."

Jane's diaries about chimpanzees

After that day, David Greybeard
often visited the camp. He allowed Jane
to get near to him in the forest, too.
He even took bananas from her hand.
Over many months, David's whole
family began to trust her.

David opened up his world to Jane.
One morning, she saw him sitting on
a red termite mound. He was trying
to get at the tasty termites inside.

Chimpanzee art

In the 1950s, researcher Desmond Morris taught some chimpanzees to paint. He hoped to find out more about chimps by studying their art.

David picked up a thin twig and stripped off its leaves. He poked it into a termite tunnel and pulled it out carefully. The twig came out covered with termites. David had made and used a tool, just like humans do. What a discovery! ❖

A glimpse of hope

Who is Birute?
More than 30 years ago, Birute Galdikas went to Indonesia to study orangutans. The Indonesian government helped her set up a sanctuary for rescued orangutans in the Tanjung Puting Reserve.

A small canoe wove silently through an inky black swamp. Above, ramin trees formed a tangled canopy. In the canoe, Birute and Arji listened carefully. The forest sounded so normal. Macaque monkeys chattered as they swung through the trees.

Map of Indonesia

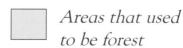

Areas that used to be forest

Areas of remaining forest

Much of the forest has been destroyed by illegal logging.

Suddenly, loud chainsaws echoed through the peaceful forest. Illegal loggers were carving their way toward the swamp.

"Is this where you saw her?" Birute asked Arji.

"Yes," Arji replied. "But we'll never get to her from the canoe. Let's walk."

They were looking for a creature high in the trees.

A shrinking habitat

Eighty percent of Indonesia's natural forest has been cut down. The wood is made into pool cues, furniture, and ornaments.

The chainsaws stopped. A logger called out, "Timber!" The trees fell, cracking and thudding on the forest floor. Then, there was a feeble, frightened grunt. Birute and Arji looked up.

"We've found her!" whispered Arji. "What luck! There's still no sign of her mother. Was she frightened by the loggers? This ape must be very weak."

Birute stood very still and called out like a female orangutan. The lonely baby orangutan responded and began to climb down from her tree. A small, red, furry arm wound around Birute's

neck and a tiny hand gripped her arm. Shyly, the trembling baby settled on Birute's arched back, just as if Birute were her mother.

Arji and Birute returned to the canoe with the baby orangutan. Overhead, a sudden crash made them all duck. Arji lifted his head slowly. Two huge adult male orangutans were wrestling and slapping each other in a frenzy. Their thick jowls wobbled with rage. They were fighting over territory. Their forest was shrinking fast.

Birute, Arji, and the baby orangutan set off for the orangutan sanctuary in the canoe. Suddenly, Birute saw a handsome orangutan darting through the trees. She recognized him.

"It's Harry!" she whispered. When Harry was a baby, he had been saved, too. He grew up in the sanctuary, and Birute released him back into the wild. There was hope for this frightened baby in her arms.❖

Smart apes

Who is Sue?
Sue Savage-Rumbaugh has studied bonobos for 30 years. At Great Ape Trust in Iowa, Sue works with Kanzi, a bonobo, who can link ideas by using a series of pictures. Kanzi communicates using 384 symbols.

Paul Raffaele stepped out of his car and gazed at the building. "Was this really America's largest great ape research center?" thought the journalist.

"Hi!" said Sue, a scientist. "It's like an ape palace isn't it? It's a great place to study apes, too. Let me show you our bonobo center."

Paul watched the bonobos swing and chase each other around the playground. He laughed as they slurped water from drinking fountains, but it wasn't anything he hadn't seen before.

Sue then led Paul to a shiny kitchen.

"Here's where the bonobos make their snacks," Sue said casually.

"Make their snacks?" Paul repeated. He stared as a bonobo warmed some food in a microwave. Now, he had something to report!

Bonobos in the wild

Bonobos live in groups in the forests of the Democratic Republic of Congo in Africa. They were only confirmed as a separate species from chimpanzees in 1929.

"So, are bonobos really intelligent," Paul asked Sue, "or do they just copy us?"

"Come and meet Kanzi," Sue replied. "He's our star. He does a lot more than just copy."

Paul gazed at the ape through a thick glass window. He was playing ball with a smaller bonobo, Nyota. Kanzi didn't look that smart.

A visitor greets Kanzi inside the research center.

"Let's go in and meet them," said Sue.

As they entered the room, Kanzi beat his legs and grunted loudly at Paul. Paul grunted back. This was scary, but fun!

"Kanzi!" said Sue. "Tell Nyota to choose a movie."

Kanzi made some sounds. Nyota thought for a while, then he pressed a key on an electronic touch pad. A movie started to play on a screen. Paul was truly amazed.

Paul listened as Sue talked about her research, which had explored the different ways that apes and humans learn. Kanzi was the first ape to show real understanding of spoken speech, learning the language in the same way as a human child.

Paul now had all he needed to write his report. He said goodbye to Kanzi and looked into his eyes.

"Hmmm," said Paul. "You're very good at getting what you want, but can you really figure things out for yourself?"

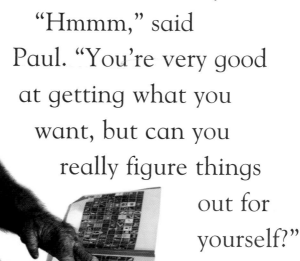

Kanzi and Sue communicate using lexigrams.

Paul left the ape complex and looked up at the cloudless sky. "I wonder if Kanzi could ever talk about the weather," he thought. ❖

War or peace?

Many scientists believe that bonobos are gentler than chimpanzees. But they have noticed that bonobos get angry sometimes when provoked.

Apes in a safe place

Who is the rescue team?

The Pingtung Rescue Center in Taiwan, supported by Monkey World in England, searches for apes, such as gibbons, being illegally sold in Asian markets. They work with the police to rescue the apes.

Black clouds sulked over the streets of Bangkok, Thailand. The air was still and sticky, but Kim, Yu, and the rest of the team from the rescue center didn't notice. They walked briskly through the crowded market, searching.

The rain came. Huge drops crashed on the tin roofs of the market stalls.

Hunted

Hunters snatch small apes from their natural habitats. The apes' mothers try to protect their young, but the hunters kill any adult apes that get in their way.

"I can hear something!" yelled Kim above the noise of the pelting rain. "I think it's a gibbon calling. It's coming from over there, behind that maze of buildings."

A bustling market in Bangkok

The team turned into a narrow alley and followed the wailing cry.

"At the end!" shouted Yu above the crashing rain. "I can see the bottom of a cage under some plastic."

The team members slowed down and pretended to laugh and joke among themselves. Yu approached the stall operator with a smile.

"Hi!" he said. "My friends and I are looking to buy a pet gibbon. Do you have any?"

Lar gibbons

Illegal markets

Many apes are transported a long way to illegal markets where they are sold as pets or for entertainment. Gibbons from Vietnam are found in Thailand.

"Yes, under this cover!" the operator snapped, looking around nervously. "Take a quick look. The police are everywhere today."

The team lifted a ripped plastic cover and peered underneath. They were shocked to see cages full of frightened, hungry animals. Two small, shivering lar gibbons crouched in the corner of one cage. The team was angry but no one wanted to startle the operator.

Yu forced a smile. "Not quite what we wanted," he told the man. "Maybe we'll come again another time."

The team left quietly. They were very upset, but they would make a proper report and then a rescue team would come to save the gibbons.

The team climbed into a truck and jerked through the crowded streets. They headed northwest out of the city to the emerald hills of Thailand.

Kim drove up a rocky trail and stopped at Wat Don Moun, a large Buddhist monastery.

A Buddhist monastery in Thailand

The team could hear gentle bells jingling inside the temple, but there was another sound as well— the singing call of happy gibbons. These gibbons had been rescued from

illegal traders. Here at the monastery, the monks looked after them well.

"At last, we have something good to report!" Kim said, smiling. ❖

Swinging and singing
Gibbons have ball-and-socket joints in their wrists that let their hands swivel as they swing. They use songlike sounds to call to each other in the forest.

Letting go

Who is Djalta?

Djalta is a western lowland gorilla. He was born at Howletts, a John Aspinall Foundation wildlife center in England. From this center, gorillas are released into national parks in Gabon and Congo, in central Africa.

Djalta jerked his head upward. A keeper was pushing food through the wire roof of his cage. Great, supper time! The young gorilla jumped onto a pile of soft straw. His agile fingers grabbed a piece of juicy papaya that was buried in the hay. Mmmm, delicious!

Papaya

Guava

He swung around and pounced
on some nuts. Sweet and crunchy!
He found some guava. Before he could
eat it, his big friend, Kwibi, rolled him
onto his back and grabbed it!

Djalta ate well but he wasn't very
happy that night. He felt uneasy, as
if something was going to change.
His instincts were right.

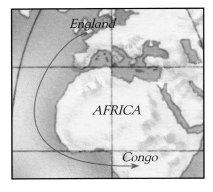

The next morning, there was a whirl of confusion. After breakfast, Djalta was led into a large truck. He began to panic, then he felt a soft slap on the head. It was his friend, Kwibi! There were also five other gorillas in the truck, which made Djalta feel a little better.

The truck started up. For three days, the young gorillas traveled, rolling along highways, gliding over water, and roaring through the air.

Finally, they were carried along bumpy roads for many miles. Then, the noise and vibration stopped. The truck door opened and a rush of warm, moist air swarmed around the gorillas.

They could hear lots of people talking. A woman's voice cried, "At last! I thought they'd never come to live with us!"

The woman held out her hands to welcome the young gorillas. "We'll work hard to help you all adapt to your new home," she said.

Djalta looked out from the truck, his eyes large and timid. He could hear birds calling and the shrill buzz of cicadas. There was forest all around and trees stretched up to the sky.

Djalta clutched the new keeper's fingers and walked into a wide clearing. He could see an enclosure, but it seemed very strange. It was made of solid logs and looked dark and spooky. He shrank away from it.

The keeper picked him up and showed him some cozy straw bedding inside a hut nearby.

"This is where you will sleep," she said softly, "until you learn how to make your own nest in the forest."

Djalta calmed down a little. There were many exciting new smells and sounds waiting for him to explore outside.

On that first day, the new keeper watched the young gorillas carefully. "It will take a long time for this group to settle," she told the other keepers. "These gorillas aren't brothers and sisters and they have no real mother. However, we must try to help them become a family in the wild."

Threats to apes

Ape habitats are shrinking fast. Some forests are being destroyed to make way for farmland. Some apes live in war-torn areas and become victims of the violence.

Djalta watched an older gorilla, Oundi, plucking some leaves. Djalta followed her for a while and began to feel bolder. He started to rummage around in the undergrowth, searching for food. For the first time, he tasted the fruits of the forest.

The young gorillas started to play together. One of them began to comb Djalta's fur with his fingers.

Gorillas eat more than 130 kinds of food in the wild.

Gorillas are gentle, sociable animals who live in groups. They communicate using gestures, vocal sounds, and facial expressions.

They still had a long way to go, of course, but slowly, these young apes would learn to live in their natural home in Africa.❖

Learning to be an ape

The keepers in the parks prepare the apes for life in the wild. They drop a wide range of food onto the straw in their huts to teach them how to forage.

Ape surprise

Who is Joe?
As a young boy, Joe traveled to many places with his parents. This trip was made 25 years ago when the family was living in northern Nigeria. There was no ape tourism then and the family felt very lucky to see an ape.

The vacation in eastern Nigeria was almost over for Tony, Catherine, and their young son, Joe. Their jeep was slowly winding its way up a steep road. The family stopped at a small turnout cut into the rock near a clear stream.

Joe dropped
a pebble into the
silvery water
and watched
the ripples run.
Suddenly, he saw a
strange reflection.

"Mom! Dad!
Look over there!"
he gasped.

Tony and
Catherine turned around.

Putty-nosed monkey

Three small putty-nosed monkeys with
long tails were waltzing from branch
to branch, moving swiftly through
the trees.

"I saw dancing monkeys!" cried Joe
with great excitement, as he climbed
back into the jeep.

The family was thrilled. They had
seen magnificent scenery on their
trip, but they had never expected
to see monkeys.

The jeep chugged on down the
mountainside. At the bottom, dense,
steaming tropical forest stretched out
around them. The air was hot
and humid now. The family bounced
along the bumpy, red-earth road.
Then an excited voice cut sharply
through the noise of the jeep.

"Oh, wow!" cried Joe. "Over there,
in the trees, is a very, *very* big monkey!"

The jeep skidded to a stop and
the family gazed at the wall of trees
by the road.

"That's not a monkey," cried
Catherine. "It's a gorilla!"

The Cross River gorilla is the rarest type of gorilla and is listed as "critically endangered." The total population may be fewer than 300 gorillas. They are only found around the border between Cameroon and Nigeria in Africa. Taking photos of them in the wild is extremely difficult, since they are rare and very wary of humans.

Apes or monkeys?

Apes and monkeys may look alike but there are important differences. For example, only monkeys have tails, and apes have bigger brains, which helps them make tools.

She was right. An enormous Cross River gorilla was leaning against a tree. He stared at the family for a moment, watching them intently.

Helping apes

Today, responsible tourism and visits to sanctuaries help raise awareness of apes and their environments. The money raised goes toward saving the apes.

Then he gripped a tree trunk with his strong arms and propelled himself away into the forest.

No one spoke for a while.

"He was special, wasn't he?" Joe whispered. "And now he's gone, just like magic."

Tony started the engine of the jeep. They moved off in silence, totally starstruck. The best presents are often the ones not asked for. This amazing gorilla was the greatest surprise ever. ❖

Glossary

Bonobo
A small great ape with long arms and black hair that lives in the rain forests of the Democratic Republic of Congo.

Endangered
Refers to a species in danger of becoming extinct throughout its habitat. Critically endangered refers to a species at highest risk.

Forage
To search and browse for food.

Gibbon
A small ape with a slender body and long arms that lives in the forests of southeast Asia.

Habitat
The natural environment where an animal lives.

Illegal
Refers to an action that is not allowed by law.

Lexigrams
Symbols that represent words. Lexigrams are used in ape-language research projects to communicate with bonobos and chimpanzees.

Sanctuary
A place where animals are protected from being attacked.

Savannah
An area of grassland with a few trees in tropical and subtropical areas.

Siamang
A very agile, large black gibbon that lives in the jungles of Sumatra and the Malay Peninsula.

Subtropical area
A region with a slightly cooler climate than a tropical area.

Termites
Pale-colored social insects that feed on dead plant material.

Territory
An area defended by one or more animals as a home base.

Tropical area
A region located near the equator with a hot and humid climate.

Ape conservation Web sites:
In 2001, the United Nations Environment Programme set up the Great Apes Survival Project (GRASP) to work with governments and local communities to save the great apes and their habitats from extinction: www.unep.org/grasp/index.asp
The Wildlife Conservation Society (WCS) saves wildlife and wild lands. Since 1996, WCS has been involved in the conservation of the critically endangered Cross River gorilla: www.wcs.org
The Ape Alliance brings together more than 40 ape-conservation organizations, and their Web site leads to many other sites about apes: www.4apes.com

Index